POST-

ALSO BY WAYNE MILLER

POETRY COLLECTIONS

The City, Our City

The Book of Props

Only the Senses Sleep

TRANSLATIONS

Zodiac
   by Moikom Zeqo

I Don't Believe in Ghosts
   by Moikom Zeqo

EDITED BOOKS

Literary Publishing in the Twenty-First Century
   with Travis Kurowski and Kevin Prufer

Tamura Ryuichi: On the Life & Work of a 20th Century Master
   with Takako Lento

New European Poets
   with Kevin Prufer

POST-

POEMS

Wayne Miller

milkweed
editions

Published 2016 by Milkweed Editions
Printed in Canada
Cover design by Adam B. Bohannon
Cover photos by Lisa Gilman
Author photo by Jennifer Drake

17 18 19 20   5 4 3 2

First Edition

Milkweed Editions, an independent nonprofit publisher, gratefully acknowledges
sustaining support from the Jerome Foundation; the Lindquist & Vennum
Foundation; the McKnight Foundation; the National Endowment for the Arts;
the Target Foundation; and other generous contributions from foundations,
corporations, and individuals. Also, this activity is made possible by the voters of
Minnesota through a Minnesota State Arts Board Operating Support grant, thanks
to a legislative appropriation from the arts and cultural heritage fund, and a grant
from the Wells Fargo Foundation Minnesota. For a full listing of Milkweed Editions
supporters, please visit www.milkweed.org.

LIBRARY OF CONGRESS CATALOGING-IN-PUBLICATION DATA
Miller, Wayne, 1976-
[Poems. Selections]
Post-poems / Wayne Miller. — First edition.
pages ; cm
ISBN 978-1-57131-470-3 (alk. paper) — ISBN 978-1-57131-921-0 (ebook)
I. Title.
PS3613.I56245A6 2016
811'.6—dc23   2015029240

Milkweed Editions is committed to ecological stewardship. We strive to align our
book production practices with this principle, and to reduce the impact of our
operations in the environment. We are a member of the Green Press Initiative, a
nonprofit coalition of publishers, manufacturers, and authors working to protect the
world's endangered forests and conserve natural resources. *Post-* was printed on
acid-free 100% postconsumer-waste paper by Friesens.

For Sean & Harper & Jeanne
my City

CONTENTS

[T]he past is not closed, it receives meaning from our present actions.

CZESŁAW MIŁOSZ

POST-

THE DEBT

He entered through the doorway of his debt.
Workmen followed, bringing box after box

until everything he'd gathered in his life
inhabited his debt. He opened the sliding door to the yard—

a breeze blew through the spaces of his debt,
blew the bills from the table onto the floor.

The grove of birches and, farther,
the beach of driftwood and broken shells

were framed by the enormous window—
that lenslike architectural focus of his debt.

He drove into town on the coiled springs
of his debt; when he bought fish at the market

he proffered his MasterCard. The dark woods
stretching inland were pocked by lightfilled cubes

of debt. The very words he used to describe
his surroundings were glittering facets

of debt. Each visit, we smoked on the deck
and, over drinks, he reminded me

with love and genuine pride: one day
all this debt would be mine.

POST-ELEGY

After the plane went down
the cars sat for weeks in long-term parking.
Then, one by one, they began to disappear
from among the cars of the living.

———

When we went to retrieve his
you drove the rows of the lot
while I pushed the panic button on the fob.

———

Inside, a takeout coffee cup
sat in its cradle,
a skim of decay
floating beneath the lid.
I'd ridden in his car
many times but never driven it.

———

When I turned the key
the radio
opened unexpectedly,
like an eye.

I was conscious of the ground
passing just beneath the floor—
and the trapped air in the tires
lifting my weight. I realized

I was steering homeward
the down payment
of some house we might live in
for the rest of our lives.

SWALLOWS

We place our blanket—
the child inside you
and you and I

radiating from her.
We open our books;
the arbor curls over.

Then: swallows
skimming the surface
of the field

as if on lines, glinting
like hydrofoils
cutting a bay.

Today we saw
the child move sharply
in the dark of you—

though still
just sand in a screen,
her 2-D cockpit.

And now: swallows
scratching lines
on the glass of the air.

To the child curled
in her window
of sound

we are nothing.
We watched her heart
blur and unblur—

a deepwater vent.
See the birds
skim the field, then rise

to the trees: that one,
now that one—
dozens of them

dipping and cutting
in Romantic abandon,
such flawless

precision!—
(Let's remember:
this is how they feed—)

THE FIRST YEAR

I

The new parents rose
to throw stone after stone
into the pond. The moonlight
barely touched them.

The surface erupted with sound
every time it was breached.

All those stones planted
in that pressurized dark
at the bottom of the pond,

the temperature dropping,
the water beginning to ice.

When the first stone hit
and didn't sink
they stopped their throwing

to observe the stone
still with them in the silent air.

2

Meanwhile, indiscernibly,
the water was draining
through a buried system

of pipes. They tossed their stones
onto the ice; each skittered
to an unreachable place.

That long winter,
the ice covered with stones
kept lowering—until at last

it rested on the mud
and the stones they'd thrown
those months ago. Then

the sun began to rise,
and the ice began to melt,
and it was spring.

INSIDE THE BOOK

For my daughter: these images,
these trenches of script. She keeps
reaching to pull them
from the page, as if the book
were an opened cabinet;

every time, the page
blocks her hand. They're *right
there*—those pictures
vivid as stained glass,
those tiny, inscrutable knots.

They hang in that space
where a world was built
in fits and erasures   she wants
to lift that world
into her own.

Meanwhile, *this* world
floods her thoughts,
her voice; it fills
the windows, the streets
she moves through;

it reaches into her
as the air reaches into her lungs.
Then, before we know it,
here she is with us
inside the book.

THE PEOPLE'S HISTORY

The People moved up the street in a long column—
like a machine boring a tunnel. They sang
the People's songs, they chanted the People's slogans:
We are the People, not the engines of the city;
we, the People, will not be denied.

                             Then the People
descended upon the People, swinging hardwood batons
heavy with the weight of the People's intent.

And the People surged, then, into the rows before them,
pushing the People against the blurred arcs
of truncheons, the People throwing rocks
into the plastic shields and visors,

                           behind which
the People blinked when the rocks hit, then pushed back
so the mass of People before them compressed.

In the windows above the street, the People looked down
and thought, Thank god we're not the People
trapped, now, in the confines of those bodies.

And soon the People on rooftops loaded their rifles
with wax bullets—which looked like earplugs—

which the People had produced in factories
full of People flanking machines designed by the People.

When the bullets buried themselves in the People
the People cried, Those shooters are not the People,
some piece of them has been removed—
like a fuse. The true People are a surface
that floats on the sea of our fathers—
how they buoy us! the People shouted.

But the People had grown tired of the afternoon
and released dogs into the crowd, dogs
that could not tell the People from the People;
and the People fled in all directions, back into the city,
singing with pain.
                    —And now, children,
when we meet the People in the market
how will we know them? *Their clubs and their bruises,*
their language of power.
                              What about concepts?
They fill them with bodies.
                              And weapons?
They spend hours piecing them together.

What else? *They open their mouths.*

And what else? *Nothing—they open their mouths.*
Is that wrong?
                    —Excuse me,
but what gives us the right to define them?
That's not what I'm saying.
                         Excuse me,
but aren't we, too, the People? Yes, but wiser.

But sir, how can the surface be different from the sea?

HOUSE NEAR THE AIRPORT

1

The next plane enters its final approach,
enlarging by degrees its shadow—

which warps as it combs the canopies
of leaves, the knocking veins of traffic;
it climbs and descends

the angled roofs one after the other,
falling to the yards, the streets
between them, a shadow dividing

and re-forming, a swatch of it sliding
through window after window—
through my kitchen window, where,

for a quarter instant, the room
darkens. Then the roar rolls over—
an empty wave. I hardly notice.

2

Plane like a massive firework:
upon landing, its contents sealed
those hours in the fuselage

explode into a hundred separate
rooms of the city. This happens
a thousand times a day.

3
Those strangers inhabit
not just the plane
but the shadow—which floods

how many windowed rooms?
I was in this shade as it carried you,
you were in my house

as it held me. Don't say that
means nothing, America—! To which
you reply: The flight path

painted over your neighborhood
is killing your property values—
and it's easy to calculate

with rudimentary physics
the height at which a plane ceases
to cast its shadow against the earth.

CONSUMERS IN ROWBOAT

The consumers have fallen in love—
they drink up their wine,
they slip into bed, where they tangle their hands.

Out the window the dogwoods are tousled with blooms,
big smudges of white.
In the morning, the consumers

work in the yard—he splits logs,
she paints the gate—
consumers in love in their house on the street

where the newspaper slaps like a hand to the stoop
(while they lie in their room
fearing death, fearing loss).

The consumers read books
late at night in their bed—
they don't speak of themselves in the way that we do—

they think of their lives as backroads to drive,
novels to write,
long hills to slide down.

The consumers imagine their voices as minds,
their words as their thoughts.
The consumers keep speaking

into their world,
their sentences foghorns propelled through the dark;
they're speaking and speaking

by choosing their markets,
the world passing through them
as though they were filters

(the world made of meals, nice liquor, and music).
We're here to remind them:
be good consumers,

remember your debt, the economy needs you—
you'll carry it forward
like a boat to the water;

one day you'll go rowing.
The consumers will anchor the oars in the oarlocks,
they'll steer themselves out

on a lake in summer:
consumers in love beneath double-arch bridges,
their profiles splashed

to the light-dappled surface—
their movements
too distant from us to have meaning.

POST-ELEGY

1

For four years, I kept your ashes in the trunk of my car—
they rode with me to work and back home
along the highway's greased tube of air.
Someone would say: What a perfect
American burial. Evenings, I pushed the remote
and the garage door unsealed like the door of a crematory.
Then, all night, the day's accumulated heat
slipped out of you. I never even
removed the box from its postal packaging.

2

Finally, I took the box of ashes to the beach
where once I'd watched you swim,
drunk, in the turbulent
aftermath of a hurricane. I tumped the dust
at the lip of the waves and they swallowed it up.
It was easy as that.

MARRIAGE

I was walking away.
As I moved, I knew:
you were sleeping in our bed.
I was pushing through time—
aware of it—
as I slid

toward another world
that seemed
enveloped
by the sheath
of an indecipherable hum.
Cupped

inside that moment,
I began to surface:
a sense of rising, the earth I
could feel lifting with me
toward a blurred layer
in the sky

through which the ground,
the street, the windows
passed, and—see?
I arrived at the warm
engine of you
asleep beside me.

THE NEXT GENERATION

They're gathering in the streets
and lifting themselves from the earth.
They're hovering—throwing rocks and gasoline—
they're flying through storefronts and alleys,
they're smashing plate windows to road salt.

They're lifting heavy-vested policemen
and dropping them on cars. Baton rounds
whir into their mass—landing against wounds,
then falling away. Those children

have risen into the air—lit orange
from flares and cars set ablaze—they circle
above us; we try to pull them down but they kick
and soar higher. The newscasters explain
and explain them, clutching them in language
they never would use—language that lifts them
(but they're already flying!) out of the streets.

This city's dome of light is anatomical,
a spleen, a turgid sack; inside it the buildings
are puttoed and griffined, and along the bottom
the children's graffiti musses the surface.
It glows in our window (and grows)

as I prep my next lesson, as we feed our daughter,
who smears her cuffs with applesauce.

By ten, the three of us are asleep—
and out there it's suddenly finished.
The children are back in their rooms
watching themselves when they flew
through the air—*There I am*,
they say and point to the screen.

THE MIND SLIDING

around inside the body
like a clot—now lodged
in the tapping foot, now
in the groin, now fanned out
in the hand on the book. Meanwhile
the foot still taps—what
does it have to do with anything?

———

And the sunflowers sliding past
beyond the glass; the mind
for an instant catches a path
between the rows,

then lets it go. Now a bridge—
and the water arriving to comb
the undershadow, the mind
slipping over and onward.

———

And the billow of strangers'
voices—how the mind
dips into their language

(like a nib into ink)—then
the conductor jangles past
the mind. And that face

———

in the glass—face
with the fields sliding
through it—face that is
how the mind has come
to think about itself.

LEAVING THE HOSPITAL

The world beyond the window
was no vaster
than the world inside the room,

just more diffuse. Window
like the screen
of an imaging machine—

on the other side:
luminous, shifting cavities.
(*Stop moving*, I said.)

You looked at me
as though I were an aquarium.
But I was a fist

forced up inside my skull
with no room to unclench.
The nurses

tended to my swollen
bags of saline—lightfilled
syrup, already part of my body,

hanging there.
When they untethered me
at last, I suddenly

was simplified. The doorway
at the end of the long hall
opened onto this

beautiful declivity: my body
was tucked back into me.

A BIT ABOUT THE SOUL

Little fuse. Little blip. Little ball of snow.
Little packet of heroin
egged inside him
(though how could he know?).

And when it burst on the airport shuttle—
like a timer going off—
well, that was his moment
next to the jumble

of luggage. How little it had to do with you
who'd sat beside him—
though now the story
of his dying breaks through

its capsule, leaking
suddenly outward. Little trigger
pulled—and you feel it
inside you, speaking.

THE AFFAIR

1

It was a desire to jump narratives—to find himself suddenly
encircled by different lights in the distant hills.

To find the hum of the engine
conveying him forward had altered its tone.

The self *had* to be asserted against that which seemed
merely given: the body's untranscendable location—

to step outside it, outside what was visible
in the mirror in the room.

2

He found himself threaded through the mouth
by his only narrative, the body that held it

propelling him forward, the light of that narrative
reaching out to strike the ground before him

in his only voice.

PRAYERS (W/ANSWERS)

I was alone in the midnight field.

I was off in the distance, watching.

Through the trees, the campfire
made a nest of light.

I like that you showed me that—
and your friends,
who swung around it.

I peeled back an ear of corn for you.

Beneath the silk, the crowded mouth,
which I like.

And weeks later, in Fitter's Bar—

I like how the light misted your hair.

Remember my beagle
sliding around on the hardwoods?

Her skin was loose,
like a costume. I like that.

And the seagulls in the harbor?
I ate fried squid by the rail.

I like the scene—
I wish I could have joined you.

I'm a little embarrassed
you saw me riding that Jet Ski.

It made a wind
only for you. That's why I like it.

I showed you Nags Head from the lighthouse.

I was there once. I like
to imagine our eyes locked into the air's
same sockets. To see it from inside you.

And the railroad bridge behind my childhood—

Your last trip home—
which, though I know you were sad,
I like.

Will you ever stop watching?

You'd have to throw me away.

And when I die?

Already you're in the archive—
this heaven resting on the living.

REPORT FROM THE PROVINCES

I can say that those stationed here
conduct themselves well—

above all else
we are citizens of the city.

We patrol the dunes,
then at night we tilt downward

to the flints in our Zippos,
to the pixel grids

pouring the city through the light
of our quonsets. Citizens

remain citizens: we persist
in our obsessions,

our minute grievances. By the fire
we voice ourselves

into the echoing
of each other's mouths. And when

the city descends
to touch us, the city

hanging taut from silk jellyfish,
we tear open the boxes

to immerse ourselves
in those spoils

that collect us—our past sealed,
we swear, inside

the slabs of the city. Soon
it's night again: the wind

drags sourcelessly over
and we huddle closer to our fuel.

At dawn, as the manual demands,
we sweep whatever

sand the night has blown in
back out through the door.

IMAGE: POSTMODERNITY

Then we were all in the cab of the snowplow

pushing across that expanse
where the city had thinned to highway.

Our headlights drew the swarm
from inside itself—not flakes, but a unified

precipitate of silence. Behind us
the city was flooded by the same

roaring body of snow. Highway
given back to the fields, traceable

by the guardrail's enclosure.
We drew ourselves along it.

Where the blade scraped the road
sparks scattered into the accumulation

that would put them out.

POST-ELEGY

For that blank half hour on the platform

the falling snow made a screen
beyond my little shelter

with its line of benches,
thin odor of manure in the air—a constant

through which the flakes slid. Below,

the rails lifted two bars of snow
above the white rind encasing the ground.

I could still picture the doctor

unzipping your abdomen—
as though your body were a suitcase.

When the train arrived, finally,

it crushed those bars beneath its wheels
all the way home for seventy miles.

ON LANGUAGE

—for Jeanne

1

There were only certain stones

                    we could step on to cross the river.

2

The stones we could step on to cross the river

                            were not certain.

3

It was difficult to decide if the stones were part of the river
or a scattered resistance to the river.

If the stones were form or content

                    inside the greater form of *river*.

4

Mainly the stones we stepped on

                        dropped away behind us
like the notes of a song.

5

A lovely village lay across the river—
but we spent most of our time focused on the stones.

When at last we arrived at the muddy bank, the village
had shifted impossibly

                              back across the river.

6
Love, stay with me inside this syntax of the river.

7
At times, the stones we stepped on
were at the bottom of the river. When we emerged—

our bodies no longer sails in the current—

the stones had risen
                              like balloons to the river's ceiling.

8
Those days, the river
                    filled our clothes, our ears, slicked us
like a dream.

9
We sat on the shoreline and looked back
across the river
                              we again would have to cross.

Looking, too, was a kind of crossing.

10

Inside the forever-descending current of the river,
a countermoving archipelago of stones.

11

Stones that, we discovered, crossed the river.

12

We spent our days crossing and crossing the river.

A BREATH IN THE RECORD

(1806 ... 1912 ... 2009)

Down in the record's
spiraling thread

the *Titanic*
has sunk, Madero

is president
of Mexico. Sun

Yat-sen's
Chinese Republic

has blotted out
the patterns

of the Qing Dynasty.
In Tyler, Texas,

Dan Davis
has been burned

at the stake.
The Olympics

are over,
Tiger Stadium

is open! These
are always the case—

———

while down in the record's
spiraling thread

sixty-two musicians
are cramped

inside a blank
studio, their instruments

nearly touching,
positioned toward

the whirlpool
of the recording horn.

The opening
chord is dominant

———

and inside each note
(a floating seed)

the fourth Peace
of Pressburg

is a canopy
over Austria,

the Cherokee Treaty
of Washington

is signed. Cape
Colony is British,

a sky of water
fills the Pontcysyllte

Aqueduct,
Lewis and Clark

have turned
toward home.

―――

Below the Leonore
Overture No. 3

is the Leonore
Overture No. 2—invisible

through the milky
blur of silence

between them
(blur of the world

in motion). While
these notes—pushed

through the screen
of an afternoon

in a white room
in May (a fire

will burn
Constantinople)—

hover here inside this
the moment

of the poem
(Bill Clinton

is on a plane
from Pyongyang,

Orly Taitz
fills the news).

———

Then—right there—
we can hear

one flautist take a breath—
just an instant

———

before the same air
rushes out and over

the lip of the mouthpiece,
down through

the silver tube
and into the chord

lifting now
from the orchestra—

a held tonic.
His body expanding

around that one
brief second

sealed in the spiral—
that gulp

the Overture surrounds,
too, like a body

becoming
the voice of a flute,

a filament of what
we've come

to think of
as Beethoven.

————

That exhale
rushing into the note

sheathes the musician
in pure sound—

while his inhale
mars the Overture;

it's not the music,
though it's held

by the music
and holds

the music inside it.
That suck of air

———

having surfaced among
the hiss, the notes—

that captured breath
sealed like a face

in the light
of a flash—that air

having risen
from the vaster

page of breath
the Overture

paves over—
that page filled,

now, with a charge
of roomlight—

———

And the notes
hang there

and hang there, backlit
for us
        here

in the window
before them.

ALLEGORY OF THE HOUSE

When it was clear there was nothing left
between us and the valley's flooding—
that even nature had come to live
inside the body of the State—

we surrounded the house in a raft
of logs and plastic barrels, cut the pipes
that bound us to the stone foundation,
and waited. On the second day

the river came over the flood bank
like an endless, unraveling cloth
and slid down into the family grove.
At first, the house just sat there,

water climbing its sides. Then
we felt the structure loosen,
and the scene that had filled my window
all my life began to tilt. Those ancient,

familiar elms drifted to the right
and disappeared—but soon
the house caught hard against them,
and for three days more we rose

precariously up their side, Sis and I
pushing back with an oar
to keep the branches
from swamping us. Next morning

we found the house triumphant
atop the water. We'd become
the tallest thing, sailing softly
over the space in which we'd lived.

Each night I lie in bed and watch
my window hold the moving world—
all of it unlocked and turning. I know
our ancestors are heavy seeds

buried in that fiction below the surface,
but the shoreline slides around
and past as though we're a compass—
and how can the earth beneath us,

the liquid air rolling across
our presence, ever be still again?

POST-ELEGY

In the image that recurred
—of a house catching fire
in the middle of a hard freeze—
I was sure you were the house.

———

Now I see
you were the fire filling the house
with motion, your light opening
the rooms from the dark,
paling the oak's curve
like the inside of a forearm.

———

When the trucks arrived
scraping their sirens
up the line of porches,
you were already
feathering at the soffits.

The men locked their hoses
to the vast reservoir
floating beneath the city

and pushed that weight against you
until at last you were swallowed
back into the blackened lath.

———

I woke to find the house sealed
in great slicks of ice—waxen
layers on the windows and walls.
I passed it each day.

Once, I went over
to look through the ice
sheeting the bedroom window:
a few of your books
lay unburned on the table
by the bed, which still
had the covers pulled back.

———

No—you must have been
the house. Those books
were yours, the shoeprints
in the snowcrust were mine.

———

But you were also the fire
that swallowed the house
from the inside—that the house
swallowed into itself—.

———

When the thaw finally came

the sun filled the street
between us with fire.

LANDINGS

I

The window of the room
in which I'm writing
(and this is true) is propped open
by the heavy book
The History of the World.

2

Written beneath the derma
of our houses:
Tyvek Tyvek Tyvek.

3

The animal writhing in the net
knows one thing:
it is *not* the net.

4

Wearing shoes, I step
against the same patch of material
over and over,
though I am moving.

5
For days, we've spoken
into his comatose body—

imagining his mind
in the shape of a target.

6
Those four buzzards
sailing like kites

anchored to a kill beyond the trees—.

7
When the dog refuses to return
the ball I've thrown

she keeps for herself
not the ball, but the field.

8
At what point does the transplanted
organ become part of him?

At what point in his mind?

9
When her finger
lifts from the piano key
the key rises

to close that space
opened
by both the finger

and the note.

10
Chords, like ladders, work
because of their emptinesses.

11
After the storm had passed
the wind kept gusting—

so rain fell only under the trees.

12
I climbed into the bell tower—
confined by air,
far removed from the city.

Then the bell began to ring.
I was suddenly
at the city's very center.

13
All branches are weightless
until they come down.

14
Each of us wearing a world
like a hoop skirt.

(And how awkward
it is to bump hoop skirts!)

15
When the movie begins
it erases the empty screen.

16
The cup on the dead man's counter
holds the charge of his thought

that he would pick it up again.

17
The coating of dust
on your eyeglasses

marks not the time since you died
but since I put them down.

18
The moth keeps ringing
against the lightbulb—

it must have the sensation
that light itself is material.

19
Ghosts have no connection
to the dead. Ghosts
are merely ours.

20
When it enters the pan
the squat pat of butter, too,
condescends to glide.

21
The dead tumble forward
like pebbles, the world

abrading them—
revealing new layers

and striations—
until they disappear.

22
It's good to remember:
butterflies
will sip blood from an open wound.

23
Watermelons are full of rain.

BALLAD (AMERICAN, 21ST CENTURY)

That spring, the shooter was everywhere—
    shot from our minds into the hedgerows,
the pickup beds and second-floor windows,
    the hillocks and tentacled live oaks. And sometimes

he was tracking us with the dilated
    pupil at the tip of his rifle. His bullets spun
into the theater's stop-sign faces, the tessellated
    car lots beyond the exits; they tore holes

in our restaurants and vinyl siding, those fiberglass
    teacups we clamored into at the county fair.
Though you don't remember it, Little Bear,
    a bullet crossed right in front of your car seat—

then window glass covered you like bits
    of clouded ice, and the rain came pouring in
as I raced for shelter at the Wendy's off Exit 10.
    Every night we kept our curtains drawn,

and while your mother slept I sat alone
    in the bathroom dark watching the news surface
into the ice-cut window of my cell phone.
    They said the shooter was in Saint Louis

shooting up a middle-school gym, then
　　he'd gone to the beach, where he killed a girl
pouring sand from a cup into a sandwich tin.
　　(Nevertheless, I pictured his face as a cloud

of insects hovering in the blackest corner
　　of the empty lot across the street.) At work
they walked us through scenarios—what to throw
　　if he came through my classroom door,

how to arm the students (desks!)
　　for counterattack. And when he came—
and when those next four people were erased—
　　they trapped him in a high-speed chase

toward the touchless car wash, where the cops
　　encircled him and, rather than relent,
he put his rifle barrel to his mouth like the mouth
　　of a test tube from some childhood experiment.

HOAX BOMB

Then our attention turned
to the package beneath the bridge.

Its dominion was absolute
and silent as a poem. Images
blew outward and everywhere.

Only narrativeless nature
could ignore it. Soon
a mechanical insect approached

on delicate tread, prodded
mysteriously, offered a report.
We were grateful, of course,

to learn the package was nothing—
that the bridge would still
funnel us, evenings, to the park.

When the man in the bombsuit
lifted the box from the embankment,
most of the people

already had left. It was removed
to a disposal center, where investigators
tore it apart,

then sifted the remains
like children through scraps
of wrapping paper.

SOME NOTES ON HUMAN RELATIONS

We pulled the rope around the neck
to squeeze the mind

    Then we had no mind

We turned the faucet of the garrote
to stanch the air

    Then we had no air

We pulled the handle
so the blade's weight split the breath

    Our breath was split

We lit ourselves on fire in the square

    The fire couldn't last forever

We stood across the field
and pulled the row of triggers

    The burlap target covered our heart

We knew we were hiding
off in the trees

      We watched helplessly from the trees

We tied together two bodies in the river
and shot just one of them

      We pulled each other under

We used a thousand cuts

      We were quaint—and merciless

We said repeatedly:
This is what the Father wants

      In the end we said:
      This is what the Father wants

We tipped the body upside down
and sawed from crotch to jaw

      Our head kept filling with blood

We threw the body from the plane
into the flat ocean

We became the ocean

In the still house
we listened to our favorite record

The chorus always killed us

The music made an ocean around the table

We sat on both sides of the table

IMAGE: PSYCHOTHERAPY

The ship is so close to shore
it seems ridiculous it can't be righted.
Every day it slips a little more.

The rooftop pool has poured its water
into the sea. The stacks' mouths
dip below the tide—water

inside an engine already underwater.
It feels like I should be able
to reach out and shift the rudder

on its massive hinge, lift the ship
back into its buoyancy. Even here—
on this shelf past the lip

of town—it's impossible
to have any real sense of its scale.

21ST CENTURY MUSEUM

The people enter
but do not know they've entered.

The café, too, is an exhibit.

When we dine we are clearly
not the art. (Whether the food is

is an excellent question—
around which a panel will coalesce.)

Closed-circuit televisions
open onto other rooms

within the building—rooms
that are unreachable

to those who bought a ticket.
When a bomb goes off

on one of many screens
the gathering audience gasps.

The whole structure rests
on a sturdy foundation

of ice. The black beyond the windows
we pin our language to

hovers one degree
above freezing. Words

like embers—impossible to tell
if they're floating in the distance

or clinging to the glass,
listless as moths. Move along,

the guard will say—
though if you stop to listen

you can hear our science
exhaling toward us,

for which we must be grateful.

FOR HARPER, 20 MONTHS OLD

I imagine your sleep
as a flashlit tent

in the narrow dark
of your room—

and when your beam
slides suddenly

across the nylon
we hear you stir.

———

Through the monitor
you come to us

aerated
like tap water.

You're dreaming—

and the unknowable
reservoir

of you
becomes in that moment

more clearly
unknowable—

and fills our room
with sound.

ALLEGORY OF THE BOAT

A boat was approaching

in a black so full the mast light felt
like a floater in the eye—.

———

Sis and I sat in the window guessing
at who this could be, what they were saying
right now, how they imagined us;

we invented their conversations
on the deck, their excitement gathering
toward our dim nub of land
in that vast, unleveling sky-over-sky.

———

In the morning, we'd go down
to the dock, see the boat up close,
press our hands to the name on the transom.
We'd find the crew

surfacing from their dreams,
beg them to draw their worlds toward us
like the cosmic lights on a passing liner.

We'd replace the crew we'd imagined
with their presence before us, speaking
themselves forward against us—

———

and then the light was gone.

Downstairs, Mom and her friends
tinked their cups, a record was playing.
I stared into the night, determined

to pull the light back into being,
but—nothing. All that time it seems
the boat had been sinking.

                              All that time
we'd imagined them trimming the sheets,
sipping their rum, talking of us,

they'd been crying out
for themselves, bailing water
as it rose around their vision of land
(our land) that had almost saved them.

———

Now what could we have done,
who should we have told? (We were up
after curfew.) Years later
that spot burned into the dark

would appear at a great distance,
drifting on an ocean of sleep.

POST-ELEGY

You were the vanishing point
where the painting pinched shut.

I stood before it for months.
People came and went behind me—

sometimes they bumped into me,
their voices flashing like mirrors.

The skylights lifted and lowered
the room as though on a pulley,

your assemblage of colors
dipped with each passage of clouds.

When, finally, I turned away,
there was still the long walk out

through those marble halls,
past thousands of paintings

lined up so perfectly their details—
their emanations—disappeared

into their collective symmetry.
The building was empty. My steps

echoed outward from my core
to be caught by the canvases,

the tapestries, the drapes
and cushioned benches

along the balustrade. The guard
in the arched entranceway

nodded vaguely, held there
by his flickering screens. Then

I was out on the street.
It must have just rained—the trees

in the arbor were heavy and slick,
the pavement stained.

And all the cafés were mottled
with people, conversations filling

the air between them. I was thirsty,
I realized, lonely and ravenous.

ON BREATHING

1

Now, again, this entire city rises and falls.
Driving the crankshaft, the flywheel,

our chests rise and fall—. Look out the window,
a few names etched in the glass: seems like forever

the city's been idling here, engine humming into the rails
when all of a sudden: Look! We're moving!

2

Last week my neighbor was shot behind the Eastsider.
I imagine him running from door to door—

as I hear he did—his breaths unthreading like a necklace.
Now those breaths seem like the only breaths

there were in the city at that time—though,
of course, we all were breathing.

3

How quickly can the engine go?
City of breath, city of air—

where does the sky begin? *Above those ginkgoes*
is where I lived as a boy—before the building came down.

My room: that quadrant of air
that had passed through my lungs, holding their stain—.

4
And you in your anesthesia sleep
beneath the windowed drape sheet—not even your breathing

can be recognized as you. And still
the city rises and falls, a diving bell

finding its level. The silvery air inside it
contracts and expands like mercury.

5
Look: the sky begins

just above the ground. The planes ascend
and descend like breaths, the chimneys

unravel into the falling snow. Last night
the player's air poured from the trumpet

like a river—narrow smokefilled room,
that river surging through it.

River of sky.

6
Walking home, I exhaled hard
against the plate window

of Murphy's abandoned filling station.
This morning, in feathers of frost,

that breath was still there.

ENVOI

Now *you*. Keep walking away
                                    from the body

you killed—
                    that died—that now

you find
            you're tethered to. The line

at your waist
            hangs slack for days,

drags in the sand,
                        dampens in the stream

so the dust
            cakes onto it. You stop

thinking about it.

———

When the line snaps tight,
                            finally, the body

pulls back
            against you, alive again—

its path scraping forward
                        in your direction

(a sustained articulation). That weight

is yours—the body, yes,
                        and the blankets

you piled on
            to cover its face,

you told yourself, to honor it.

NOTES

The Miłosz epigraph is from "What I Learned from Jeanne Hersch," trans. Czesław Miłosz and Robert Hass.

All the Post-Elegies are for—though not necessarily about—my father, Wayne C. Miller, 1939-2008.

"The Next Generation": e.g., the majority of rioters during the 2013 Belfast, Northern Ireland, "flag protests" were under eighteen. Reportedly, many would go home just before 10:00 p.m. so they could see themselves on the news.

"Prayers (w/Answers)": In October 2012, it was announced that Facebook had passed one billion active users.

"A Breath in the Record": One of the first orchestral pieces recorded for the phonograph was Beethoven's Leonore Overture No. 3, composed in 1806, recorded in 1912. The piece had to be arranged for a smaller ensemble, since a full orchestra wouldn't fit inside the recording studio. The poem was written in August 2009 and is dedicated to Jake Adam York.

"Landings": *The History of the World*, by J. M. Roberts. Tyvek is a strong, high-density fiber used as an insulator housewrap, trademarked by DuPont. . . . *condescends to glide*—from Rainer Maria Rilke's "The Swan," trans. Stephen Mitchell.

ACKNOWLEDGMENTS

Thanks to the following publications, where these poems first appeared, sometimes in different versions: *Barn Owl Review*: "The Debt"; *Bear Review*: "For Harper, 20 Months Old" and "Leaving the Hospital"; *Boulevard*: "Report from the Provinces" and "Two Consumers in Rowboat"; *The Cincinnati Review*: "Marriage"; *Conduit*: "House Near the Airport" and "Prayers (w/ Answers)"; *Copper Nickel*: "A Breath in the Record" and "Post-Elegy [In the image that recurred]"; *Crazyhorse*: "The Mind Sliding" and "Some Notes on Human Relations"; *Descant*: "Allegory of the Boat"; *Field*: "Post-Elegy [You were the vanishing point]"; *Granta Online*: "Post-Elegy [After the plane went down]"; *Gulf Coast*: "Image: Psychotherapy"; *Handsome*: "Hoax Bomb," "Landings," and "The Next Generation"; *Indiana Review*: "The People's History"; *iO*: "Allegory of the House" and "21st Century Museum"; *The Kenyon Review*: "The First Year"; *Low-Ball*: "A Bit about the Soul" and "On Breathing"; *Ploughshares*: "Inside the Book" and "On Language"; *Poem-a-Day* (The Academy of American Poets): "The Affair"; *Raleigh Review*: "Ballad (American, 21st Century)" and "Image: Postmodernity"; *The Southern Review*: "Envoi," "Post-Elegy [For four years I kept your ashes]," and "Post-Elegy [For that blank half hour]"; *West Branch*: "The Swallows." *Poetry Daily* reprinted "Post-Elegy [In the image that recurred]" and "Prayers (w/Answers)"; *Verse Daily* reprinted "Report from the Provinces." *Language Lessons: Volume I* (Chet Weise and Ben Swank, eds.; Third Man Books, 2014) reprinted "Allegory of the House," "A

Bit about the Soul," "The People's History," "Post-Elegy [After the plane went down]," and "Some Notes on Human Relations."

Thanks to Kevin Prufer, Brian Barker, and Joy Katz, who read this book in manuscript and offered invaluable edits and advice. Thanks to Daniel Slager, Patrick Thomas, and the rest of the extraordinary people at Milkweed Editions. Thanks to the US-UK Fulbright Commission and Queen's University Belfast for a Fulbright to Northern Ireland, where many of these poems were written. Thanks, too, to my colleagues at QUB—particularly Sinead Morrissey, Ciaran Carson, and Anthony Bradley. Thanks to the University of Central Missouri and the University of Colorado Denver for supporting my work. Thanks to the following people, who in various and important ways made this book possible: Benjamin Johnson, Hadara Bar-Nadav, Kathryn Nuernberger, Nicky Beer, Randall Mann, Michelle Boisseau, Sean Hill, Alex Lemon, D. A. Powell, John Gallaher, Murray Farish, Marc McKee, Martha Serpas, Audrey Colombe, and Paul Perry. Thanks, too, to friends and supports in Belfast, particularly Andy Eaton, Holly Mccomb, Stephen Sexton, Stephen Connolly, Sam Riviere, and Matthew Reznicek. Thanks to my mother and Neill. The biggest thanks, as ever, go to Jeanne.

WAYNE MILLER is the author of three previous collections of poetry: *The City, Our City*, *The Book of Props*, and *Only the Senses Sleep*. He's also a cotranslator of two books from the Albanian poet Moikom Zeqo and a coeditor of three books, including *New European Poets* with Kevin Prufer and *Literary Publishing in the Twenty-First Century* with Travis Kurowski and Kevin Prufer. The recipient of the Bess Hokin Prize, the George Bogin Award, and a Ruth Lilly Fellowship, as well as a finalist for the William Carlos Williams Award and the Rilke Prize, Miller teaches at the University of Colorado Denver, where he edits *Copper Nickel*.

Interior design and typesetting by Adam B. Bohannon

Typeset in Adobe Caslon